Black Life

Presents

Pure Love

BlackLife

Pure Love
Copyright © 2013 BlackLife

All rights reserved. Except for use in any review, the reproduction or utilization of this work in whole or in part in any form by any electronic, mechanical or other means, now known or hereafter invented, including xerography, photocopying and recording, or in any information storage or retrieval system, is forbidden without the written permission of the author, BlackLife. He can be reached at: BlackLife123@yahoo.com

ISBN: 10:0615775446
ISBN-13: 978-0615775449

Authored by Nolan J. Turner (BlackLife)
Edited by BlackLife
Cover by KRose Designs

Pure Love

Thank you

To my Lord and Savior, for always continuing to bring me a mighty long way and guiding my pen along with my heart. I would not have anything without your blessings.

Thank you

To all the wonderful people that surrounds me and have possess a piece of my heart. Without you my soul would not have sought the strength to prepare for my pure soul mate.

Thank you

Always to my left hand for holding the paper while my right hand wrote (love it!).

This book is dedicated to everyone that desires true love and who has been through the trials and tribulations yet never gave up.

Thank you....Black*Life*

INTRODUCTION

Relationships, experiences love and heartaches; close your eyes while opening your heart as Pure Love takes you on a journey of love, fantasies and heartaches. Unfortunately, every Pure Love is not pure and every soul mate does not protect your soul. Pure Love shows the ups, downs and how the heart can bounce back with faith and prayer.

Pure Love shows our heart desires and how love can conquer all. Relationships can endure problems. Showing that man and woman can offer more than just lust to one another and real love still exists.

This book express that not only women wants to be loved and appreciated but men also seeks and desires completeness as well. Pure Love gives you such pieces of work from "She loves me, she loves me not" to a more heart felt piece entitled "Angelic".

Sit back and let your fantasies become realities.

Remember these three quotes...

1. *"Remember no one deserves love more than you"* translation never let your heart be down played by another person.

2. *"Never be jealous of the time you choose to give to someone else, that you're not willing to give to yourself"* translation if you spend more time investing in someone else and you're empty inside, you did it to yourself. Therefore don't fault the receiver of your affection.

3. *"Don't let the pains of the heart road block and be your repellent from allowing true love"* translation - again, remember no one deserves love more than you......

Black*Life*

PURE LOVE

Love appears in your life when you least expect it

Coming along in all shapes, sizes and forms

We are all out here looking for our soul mate

But know that every mate is not good for your soul

Relationships are like gold

It goes up and down

Continuing to maintain value

But to get to that gold

We sometime experience fools gold

The search for happiness is worth the journey

The reward is Pure Love

And that is worth the wait

Pure Love

TABLE OF CONTENTS

Haiku (My Love)	4
Angelic	5
Love	6
Search	7
…..Walk Into My Life	9
If	11
Married	13
Remembering Love	15
Eternal Love	17
Remember You	18
Used To Love Me	19
She Love Me, She Love Me Not	21
My Gift To You	22
I'll Be	23
Feeling	25
Her	26
I Want To Love You	28
My Attempt	29
Not Perfect	30

TABLE OF CONTENTS

As One	32
My Vows	33
Simply This	34
I Was Your Moon	35
When The Smoke Clear	36
You	37
Mesmerize	38
Moments of Love	40
…She!	41
I….	43
That Night	45
Destiny	47
Wanted	48
Complete Me	50
Will You	51
Forever	53
(Bonus) Random Thoughts	55
A 10/2 Moment	56
Outro	58

Pure Love

BE INTRIGUED……

HAIKU (MY LOVE)

Yesterday we met

Today I will love you more

Tomorrow who knows?

ANGELIC

Uncommon to my nature, I felled victim to your innocence

The sound of your voice hypnotized my ear drums, resembling a baby's heartbeat

Overwhelmed by your skin tone that glow of beauty even in the mist of darkness

Reaching out to you I experienced the texture of silk

As our fingers tips connect, bonding in our forever

I've imagined this moment for awhile now

Hoping time could stand still so my moment remains everlasting

But the only one not moving is me being suspended in time

As my heart beats to the second hand

My mouth opens, vocal forming a sound that refuse to escape thy tongue

Gasping for air filtering in what seems to be your fragrance

Realizing you are not here or is it that you only existed in my mind

LOVE

Love seems to remind me of the four seasons:

Winter fills your heart with pain and sorrow like frozen trees
Weighing heavily down with icicles
Birds forced to vacate their homes with no choice
As if they're being evicted
Lakes and rivers frozen, no place for the Swans to swim and play
Pain for the homeless, cold and weary as they pray for shelter

The way I feel without you....

Spring brings a sigh of relief that it will get better
That the birds will soon sing again
Flowers are preparing to bloom
The chills will soon leave the skin of the homeless
The lakes will fill with the Swans offspring
Fresh air would fragrance the sky

And like Snow White you'll awaken to me again.....

Summer has secure my feeling on life star filled nights
Nights at the park picnics with your family
Birds chirping, ducks quaking and the smell of flowers
That enhanced your sense of scent
As you enhance the feeling of true love in the air

Restoring my ability to love....

Fall then comes around to begin the sorrow
Tree begins to wither away
Birds prep to leave their homes they have worked hard for
The homeless set out to find new shelter
The morning dew becomes morning frost built by snowflakes

And our love becomes memories of the past....

SEARCH

I had thoughts of you, me, we
Living our life, house, kids, dogs
Full reality

Paying bills, mortgage and all the
Other shit that goes with responsibility

That walk in the park shit that
Made me wanna get down on one knee

Dun picked out the perfect ring
Practicing in the mirror those words
"Will you marry me"?

Sweaty palms and shit cuz
all I wanted do for you is please you

Thought that fully clothed humping
Was your foreplay till I realize
You was just a tease

Bringing my reality to a full halt
When I discovered you was just
Playing make believe

You wanted everything but the
Title that went with being with
A real man like me

See you wanted the clothes,
Jewelry and the Direct T.V.

But wanted me in the lazy boy
Cause you didn't wanna share
The love seat

SEARCH

I should've known in your letters
When you spelled love (L.U.V.)

Your lack of maturity
A grown ass woman is what
I need who has enough time
To spell love with the O and the E

A grown ass woman who deserves
My pension and social security

Not a wanna be grown ass woman
Still residing on Sesame Street

Cuz I realized that you was all
I hope she wouldn't be

....WALK INTO MY LIFE

She's going to walk into my life and
I'm going to marry her
Delivered straight from God,
Accepting her without
The least bit of hesitation

Knowing her to be the reason I was
Born to this Earth
The reason I'm whole
For she will complete me

The greatest gift to any man
Yet I will be blessed to receive her
And each day with her will be like
A new experience, a new birth

Knowing there to be a God,
Cause for her I've prayed for
My prayers were answered
The first moment I seen her smile

She will shower her love on me,
Our heartbeats will
Combine as one,
We will create the heart of our one day child

I will honor and appreciate her
Every moment we share the same space
Giving to her my everything for she will see
Pass my mistakes and bring out my best

As her husband I will be proud to become
Proud to introduce her as my soul mate, my wife
Classy enough to be my Michelle to Barack,
But hood enough to hold it down like Bonnie to Clyde

….WALK INTO MY LIFE

I would gift to her two stars in the sky
So even after death we will continue to shine
Our love will outlast the change
Of the four seasons

And when she walks into my life
I will fulfill these words and never let her go…

IF

Look me in my eyes and tell me without me you can live

Touch my heart and tell me you don't feel us on the same beat

Taste me as I you, do you not taste the same flavor?

As you take your morning breathe do you not smell my scent?

Peacefully I speak into your ear do you not hear the sound of harmony

Is it possible that my love is in vain going to waste on you?

Do you really feel I need to shut the door on us?

Disconnecting the lines of love that has brought us thus far

Closing my eyes to see you slowly vanishing from my mind

Another idea for a used to be love song

People can say "yeah I knew that wouldn't last".

When we retire the Earth, the elders than can say

"I heard of them what a shame, a waste"

Two hearts bound to one another but refused to accept each other

Because society can't accept you and I loving one another

Maybe they're right and we're wrong or maybe they're wrong and we're right

Maybe we make each other so happy that they'll see the errors of their ways

Maybe we will listen, separate from one another by walking away

IF

Until we can't see each other in eyesight any longer

Why not, it's occurring anyway, the picture you have of me in your room

Day by day I'm slowly fading away until all you see is background

Unless you learn to believe in our unity, the one that has brought us this far

Or maybe you'll never believe in rainbows, gold, or soul mates

Maybe you don't believe in true love or you don't love me truly

Without me you can get back to a reality that's not confusing

I've destroyed before with my eagerness to love

Could you possibly have realized this?

So you got out before the end pacifying me by calling me a friend

I refuse to say I don't want to let you go and you refuse to say you don't want to go

Now as we stand on either side of the door saying "Damn" out of defeat

What do we do now?

These words have no ending just what

IF….

MARRIED

I dream one day I'll be married

And she'll make me change my thuggish ways

Be the rehab to cure me of my hoeish addiction

Realizing I'm not out just to fuck her brains out and dip

But her nightly intimate sexually energy on a journey yet known

Putting my ear to her chest as the rhythm from her heart soothe me to sleep

Shaking my head with a gleam in my eye thinking "she got me"

I just want to look her in her eyes

And say "I Love You" for no reason

Kissing the tears from her eyes when she feels sorrow

Be the one person she needs to end those rainy days

I want to rub her feet from the long days

And start her shower while she tells me

About her goals and ambitions

Wash her temples as the stress

From the hours, minutes, seconds wash down the drain

Everyday I want to in tune myself more with her soul

At night in my dream replays the memories from yesterday

Wanting to know having her in my life is all I need

MARRIED

And everything else is a special gift

The type of love that if lost in Hart Plaza, our kinetic energy will lead us back together

Glazing at the stars until I connect them in the image of her face

They say everyone has a twin but they lied because there could never be another her

And the sex game is great but wouldn't be anything without the way she stimulates my mind

Telling dudes don't be jealous of what I have

Patience and your "her" will come as mine did

See I don't need her IRA, 401K or pension

There is no price tag for the spiritual love

We've been allow to share

And when the Angels from above

Come down to take her hand

I would plead with them for a two for one

For she is my dream of being married

Without her is my nightmare.......

REMEMBERING LOVE

I've closed my eyes
Seeing the brightest of sunny autumn days
Ducks flying over head in perfect formation
Swans treading water gracefully
Like ballerinas dancing on the stage of life
Leaves fire red and orange as they
Blow off the branches

Laying on my back staring into the clouds
Pure white as snow
The smell of the fresh air so relaxing
Carrying different scents through the air
Every movement causing the leaves
To crush and crackle
Such a colorful presentation
Swirling through the air

Softly our lips kiss barely enough to feel it
But enough to feel each other's breathe
Steals each other's soul
The scent of your perfume covers
My body sending me into a trance of forever after
Exploring each other down to the finest detail
Lying on a bed of white and purple orchids
We begin to make love

Physically you fill me completely
Welcoming me into your enchanted garden
Verbally we form a duet only heard by hummingbirds
We had become as one for this time of intimacy
Mentally in sync I could sense your every thought
While straddling me you move gracefully
Like a cobra serenaded by a flute
Arched back in perfect rhythm
You created an outer body experience

REMEMBERING LOVE

The evening begins to set across our bodies

Feeling lost to the Earth we remain found in each other
Night air begin to mask the scent of love making
The chill begins to dry the sweat from our bodies

Whispers that once soothed my ears begin to fade
Visions of you I no longer can see

But the memories of love we made
Will be everlasting amongst the trees
Our sweat planted in the Earth
Love felt by Mother Nature
And moments counted by Father Time

ETERNAL LOVE

Meet me in Eternity
Rose petals blowing
Across the marble floor
Candles burning around the room

Hear the harp
Playing gently in our ears
Changing the beat of our hearts
To the tone of our love

Partaking in the fruits
We will hand feed one another
As the juices tantalize our tongues
Soothing our craving

Join me in a dance
That creates its own rhythm
As the music guides our feet
Across the floor

Swim with me like mermaids
Through the deep blue ocean
Returning to our mystical world of Atlantis
Protected from all harm

Together lets conquer
The highest mountain
Claiming this great wonder
Naming it after our love

Let us leave our bodies
And float away
As our souls meets in Heaven
Beginning our new life

REMEMBER YOU

Remember you are the one I gave my heart to
Accepting it was never a problem for you

Making me feel at ease how you open up to me
Being the golden Sun that made me well, you know

I could never stop sparkling with the thought of you
Roaming through my mind

Your image takes over my thoughts
Often clouding my every moment

I couldn't erase you if I wanted to
Constantly I remember you....

USED TO LOVE ME

She used to love me from every "Good morning" and "Baby I love you" to "Goodnight"

Or would stop by with dinner because she was concerned about my appetite

A kiss in the middle of a sentence just to show her affection

Staring at her I began to see my own image my own reflection

Valuing every moment that was made to be with each other

She was my kinetic soul mate stronger than just a friend or a lover

Creeping through the house ensuring we didn't wake the babies

Punishing the bed with our wild ways fun and just being crazy

If walls could talk they would say no one else can do it like we did

The aroma of sex like a candle when the lid is removed

From late night creeps to late night trips

Blowing I love you kisses or the way she glossed her lips

Smiling faces that used to stick in my mind all day

Or how my name rolled off her tongue in an orgasmic way

Just the sound of her breathing would relax my heart

Even when we were separate we were never apart

She was my black super woman, describing me as her weakness, her Kryptonite

USED TO LOVE ME

Slowly she was gone fading into the mystical light
Disconnected from her voice, texting and phone calls

Names that have taken place in the history of dwellings with talking walls

Kisses that blew through the wind like rose petals during the fall season

No more smiling, caressing, love making and no more pleasing

Almost like the last page torn out of a suspenseful book

Not knowing how it could have ended leaves me anxious, confused and shook

Waking up everyday to a lonely existence of how do I manage now

Roaming through a parallel world lost without any sound

But remembering how she used to love me for all my faults and flaws

I used to love her too

I just didn't tell her enough….

SHE LOVE ME
SHE LOVE ME NOT

Yesterday I brought a dozen roses while I thought of her
I remembered the first day we met
I bought a rose
With that I said….

        She love me, she loves me not

I can see it plain as day, awaiting the night response from her
As I repeated to myself

        She love me, she loves me not

As her soft lips rubbed across the petal of the rose that she received

She said so sweet and gently

        I love him, I love him not

I understood because she have been deceived
But know just now

        I love you, I love you not

So I bought a dozen roses to spread at her feet
For only the best for my Queen

        Love you, love you not

And to sprinkle in her bath water
Because a rose can truly only be scented by a rose

        Love me, love me not

For she is the rose that fulfills my garden of exotic flowers

MY GIFT TO YOU

When you are feeling let down
Allow me to pick you up and keep you strong

Feeling your pain when you are ailing
Enduring the aches that visit you monthly

Being the umbrella that protects you
From the rain that fall on your head

As your eyes close see my light
May it guide you to the truth that plagues your mind

Shielding your heart from all the stress
That hinders you emotionally and creates your heart anguish

Allow me to walk with you
So that you don't have to be alone, facing life endeavors

Shall no one ever damage our foundation
For I'll walk in front of you to ensure your protection

Together we will remain equal to one another
Never allowing our tongue to cease communication

May our eyes always see the truth in each other
Never doubting our vision

As the days progress let me be the calendar,
That marks the years that we have shared thus far

And on your journey home, may the Lord allow
me to be the breeze that softly blows
your ashes peacefully away

I'LL BE

I once saw in you what you helped me to discovered

Growing closer and closer to you as if there was no other

As your soul takes over the inner walls of my body

Gracefully feeling I can float through the sky emotionally

Thinking I knew love not realizing that I was still in training

The restlessness nights, frog in throat waiting

 anticipating your love

Heart racing as your smile takes over my smile

Seeking you out like an expedition down the Nile River

My Queen I've named you so fitting to the crown I've put on you

Thinking I've found my white picket fence surrounding my home

Constantly trying to convince me we are not right for one another

You said the devil made us do it, but God created this

We understand it so we could be soul lovers

Dreaming of your emotions making love to my emotions

Our sweat and tears creates an intimate potion

I've tried to step away respectfully and patiently for this you asked

Not knowing that within doing so my heart

Slowly became weak with a faint heartbeat

I'LL BE

Blackening, hardening, at the soul you created

Begin dying off like trees damaged at the roots

Browning and drying breaking off every time I heard

You're saying we're no longer meant

But in my heart I knew our love still existed

Until that day when you realize us

I'll lay asleep in my own fairytale

Awaiting your kiss…..

FEELING

I

Feel you even

When

You are

Hiding your feelings

And

Trying not to be

Felt

HER

She walked into my life
Filling my head with dreams of ever after
In the mist of sorrow and pain
She brought out joy and laughter

She was like the scent of Lilies
As they blow in a gentle spring wind
Light mocha in complexion, lips soft and juicy
Like a Georgia peach and big brown eyes
That drew me in

Her words flowed from her lips
In a sweet and melodic tone
She accepted me as her KING
Taking my rightful place on the throne

She was my support, inspiration
I would never fall as long as she
Was my foundation
She was like the deep blue sea
And her current pulled me in without hesitation

She made love to me taking me
Into a time warp far away from Earth
Her Solar System surrounding my Milky Way
As if we were creating a new planet

She was the blood running through my veins
For she was to me my soul mate
If taking a rib from my left side meant my demise
That was the risk I was willing to take

She was my butterfly
Protected safely in my cocoon
Comforting and reassuring as she held me
As if I was created from her womb

HER

She was my daydream in the sunrise
And my sweet dream in the moonlight
That star you close your eyes and wish
Upon with all your might

She was my reality, my fantasy, my true love
For that one moment in time
A love I couldn't keep

Cause my love
Was his
And never mine.....

I WANT TO LOVE YOU

I want to love you in a way that the world wouldn't understand
Being the new Adam and Eve
Gods' perfect plan

Living in a life measured by time nor space
Never needing another to occupy your place

Never filling a void if this day we didn't speak
Intimately we never limited our pleasures for more we would seek

Safe in my arms you would fall asleep believing in me
Secure in your heart I feel your purity

On this ride of never ending pavement
Continually thanking God for this Angel He sent

With you I can be myself hiding behind no mask
I know you to be my Ruth as I am your Boaz

The perfect Black couple, Martin and Coretta
Going down in history
Because in love we did it better

Or maybe like the Greek Gods, Hera and Zeus
Will have our own stars that people gaze at and point to

And it seems so perfect the way I want to love you

Unaccepted because…

You did not love yourself…..

MY ATTEMPT

It is my attempt to love you, like no other love on Earth

To have you hold me like I haven't been held since birth

Smiling at you with a sparkle in my eye

Holding back tears on the phone when I know it's time to say 'goodbye'

Walking into your arms feeling my knees going weak

Dreaming pleasant dreams as you lay next to me asleep

Smiling that perfect baby smile awakening with you by my side

Keeping it real able to be myself, my truth I didn't have to hide

Surrounded by your energy that helps me through my day

Not stumbling over my words because around you there's nothing I can't say

Lost in you as I stare out at the clouds

No longer feeling like a cage animal for you've returned me to the wild

So it is my attempt to love you, like no other love on Earth

A love that you've assured me has been worth the search…..

NOT PERFECT

You gave me your heart before
I knew the importance of love
Before I realized that causing you
Pain was too painful to bare

I heard your misery but was to
Selfish to acknowledge your feelings
Selfishness that only allowed me
To add salt to your wounds unknowingly

Blinded by the false perception of what
Females could offer at the moment
Not seeing the vision you tried
To share for our lifetime

I took years from you
Before you even seen it coming
Tried loving you
When you no longer wanted my love

Creating hatred I worked
Hard to get you to erase
And harder to get you to understand
The lack of my mature years

Struggling hard to become the man
I've become today
To look back, to see how far
I've came to only benefit the next

For you have chosen your course
And it doesn't include my direction
Although I've often seen you at
The intersection of life and destiny

NOT PERFECT

A lesson of everything is not meant
To be or things worked out
But everything can be repented for
And learned from

I've acquired a lot of mistakes
Along my journey in life
And I'm sure more will follow for me
I'm human and that's what I do

By no means am I perfect cause
There's no such thing
But I'm perfect at trying
To be the me I am now

And I thank you
For not giving me a second chance
Because it helped me create a better
Me…….

AS ONE

Fireflies flutter through midnight lights

Holding each other our hearts communicate as one

Often I attempted to look into your eyes to see your thoughts

Want to be in two different rooms writing identical lyrics to the same hook

Creativity that intrigues the mind

At the end of every thought your smile is what I see

Closer and closer I see you, it seems as if we are as one

I know your thoughts by the expressions on your face

Recite your words when your lips form to speak

Feeling I know you better then I know myself…

MY VOWS

Wake me up from this dream I'm experiencing

The good feeling that it sends through my body

Making me lick my lips as sweat trickle off my forehead

Heart beating uncontrollably, causing my body to shiver

My eyes to become starry, my palms moist from your beginning and my end

Goosebumps forming down my body as you soothe me

Your control over me is greater than I anticipated

I try to run but I feel stuck in your trap (Venus)

Should I attempt to stay hoping you are equal to one self (Earth?)

Mesmerized by your voice drawing me to the sea like a mermaid's song

Spiritually grounded forcing my soul to maintain faith

My growth comes from your morning dew that nourishes my shell

As you gracefully dance through my heart like Debbie Allen

With your soft voice soothing my ears like Phyllis Hyman

Knowingly outside of the Lord, I am the only other one you honor

As to you I will honor the same eternally

Combining your Sun with my Moon and together we will form an Eclipse

SIMPLY THIS

Simply this

I want to be your dream at night

and

The reason you smile in the morning

I WAS YOUR MOON

I was your moon

That made your heart race through the night

Acknowledging the animal in you fully

You craved for the moon that shadowed over your soul

When you felt loss, the glow led you to an enchanted field of lust

Piercing down on you as you dreamed of intimacy seldom reached

Creating the perfect silhouette of your bare body projecting off the land

Hiding you in the clouds that seals my brightness

Finding you in the fog in a place only we're familiar with

Greeting you in the late night covering your steps
 as you walk I follow

Hearing your orgasmic screams as if you were hollowing at me

Watching you run off before the search party come looking

Never being a suspect but always a part of your foul play

Always waiting for you in the night at the same place and time with the mist in the air

Whether quarter, half, or full moon the time spent when you looked up at me was priceless

I was your Moon

I was your Secret from..... Him

WHEN THE SMOKE CLEAR

When the smoke clear, will you protect me?
Like a cocoon does a caterpillar
Watching my growth through metamorphosis

Possessing my soul with your spirit
My heart with your blood
My mind with your thoughts

Will you walk with me?
Never forgetting to communicate or share with me
Remembering through our passionate chemistry we are bonded

Bathing my emotions with tears of happiness,
Sorrow and painful feelings

Can it be possible to feel out of body?
If so did you know that someone would with you?

My direction
My compass
Keeping my eyes focus on my journey

As the scale balance our lives together
As equal partners

Chilled by your deep blue water
Washing over my black sparkling sand
Will you remain in paradise?

Enjoying our rare Caribbean love

YOU

Will you….

Could you….

Marry me?

Be the woman of my all

As I serve only you

The lifeline that makes my heart constantly beat

The Sun that dries all the rain away

Causing the chill bumps that form when you enter my sight

The Moon of my lonely nights

A lonely man following my Northern Star

Leading me to your open heart

Will you…

Could you…

Say I do?

MESMERIZE

You mesmerize me from the color of your hair

To the style that sculpts your face

Water form in my mouth as I watch your lips

Speak with the soft pitch that flows from your vocal chords

Visiting your eyes I frequently see you and I, and I and you

Mesmerize by what you do, how you do it, when you do it

Like the way you walk with hips that sway like a breeze on a willow tree

As you stand still I've traced your outline

Through connections that give images to my brain

The light blue sky and clouds that embodies your smile

Mesmerize by your heart and its fears

The truth and the way you embrace reality

Your hand motions tapping when you're irate

And how they spread when you're relaxed

The way water rinses down your body

The imprint you leave in the bed sheets

MESMERIZE

I'm mesmerized by the outer body orgasm

That you cause me without touching

The emotions you bring to my heart

The sensation you give to my sexual manhood

By your spiritual connection continuously seeking through God

So we can be closer to one another in his heart

Creating our perfect harmony

MOMENTS OF LOVE

I want to lay you down on a bed of rose petals

Lacing your body with silk sheets

Candles burning all around the room

As I watch your silhouette off the ceiling

Warm oil dripping through the sheets

Clinging to every inch of your body

Sweet sounds of rain tapping the roof

Sharing the same rhythm of our hearts

Removing the silk from your face

Lips caressing yours rounding your lips with my tongue

Slowly removing the silk from your sculpture

The tip of my tongue moving down your shape

Until you clinch the sheets from excitement

Your heart beats faster from this experience

I clothed your body with mine

As we share a dream

……..SHE!

She's right in my face and doesn't realize
I desire her as much as
I desire my next breathe
Dreaming of our wedding day
At church were all I see is her
With all the joyful noise
But to me silence cause her voice chimes
Through my ears

Why is she so unsure of what is right?

If given the chance,
I would rest my ear to her bosom
Listening to her heart beat as mine synchronize
To the same rhythm until our souls
Are ball rooming in the moonlight

If she cooks, I will wash dishes
She does laundry, I will fold
When she showers, I will wash her back
As she dries, I will oil her completely
We will take care of each other
Till the sunsets
Upon us no longer

She smiles with innocence
That creates an instant sense of security
Never have I been so sure of anything
Other then my love for God
And the DNA of my off spring

I need her to need me as much
As I need her

……..SHE!

She's my glow from the moon
The mating sound of crickets in my misty field

The sun in my window
Providing the rays of my growth

The creation from my rib

She

Is of me…

Pure Love

I....

I want to be married
I want to kneel at the alter and give my heart
To her in front of God

Take her hand and jump the broom
Like our ancestors before us
Carrying her across our threshold

Everyday I want to
Look her in her eyes and see myself
She'll be like my twin
Putting the finishing word
On my every thought

On that day I'll become her husband
Providing for my wife and encouraging her dreams
Protecting her heart and conquering her fears

We will hold hands in the park
Watching the swans drift effortlessly across
The waters with their flock

Experiencing carriage rides, eating cotton candy
Picking flowers and just the simple things
In life that lover does

Working our jobs sharing our ups and downs
And praying together to conquer our woes

I will be her knight in shining armor
Always keeping her protected
From life wrong doers

I....

Always holding her to the standard
God has set for her while following the
Same for myself

For if we pray together it increases
Our odds of ever lasting.....

THAT NIGHT

What is it that intrigues me about you?

Is it your dark complexion that brings out your eyes?

Or your smile that shows off your sparkling whites

Your thickness that makes me thirst for a taste

The intelligence you bring to the conversation

A sense of humor that makes me star graze

Your emotion making my heart gasp

The tears I have watch you cry as pain plaque you

Let's continue to talk, let's continue to learn

Inventing the strength that makes us bond

Ropes that tie us to one another may they remain tied

May you remain true; to you I shall do so as well

To you I shall hold one night dear to my soul

The night we kiss

The night I meet all of your being

Truth, honesty, emotions, and your confessions

Never change who you are

Cause no one can ever take that from you

THAT NIGHT

That will be what's remembered when your time
Comes to become a star

Placed among the stars of Angels
That continues to shine before you

All of this I learned of you that night...

DESTINY

Destiny

Is

You

And

I

WANTED

You wanted me as your finger tips gently outlined my shoulder blades

I felt paralyzed awaiting your next caressing grip

The warmth of your body monopolized my body, like the fog over a moonlit field

Gasping for air I can feel my heart beat steadily growing

Your breast pressed against my back

Creating all the right motions you ensured my thirst for you had me dehydrated

Your soft lips pierced my spine forming chill bumps making me surrender all control

Serenading me with your voice had me lost in an enchanted forest envision in my mind

Confirming your mastery, you turned me to you

Then you kiss me softly as I felt suspended in time

Completely hypnotize from the scent of your pheromones

I have unknowingly relinquished control

Anxiously anticipating your next step I can feel the energy of our souls connecting

Full of life you've added years to a lifeline that was starting to beat with a slow pulse

WANTED

You have awaken this sleeping prince who was fool enough to bite the forbidden apple

The love you made to my soul, my spirit, and my heart

Was more orgasmic then and physical stimulant

Spinning my mind through a world wind of pleasure never felt before

You wanted me

When I needed to feel wanted the most….

COMPLETE ME....

Be the woman that God created
From my left rib

Let your words be those that complete
My every sentence

Taking our vows at the alter given thanks
To our creator for this blessing

Carrying in your womb our seed as
We partake on another saga of our lives

I want you to be the calm to my Storm
My better half to this life

Me being your BOAZ protecting and
Providing for my wife

As we nurture each other needs
And appeal to one another wants

Being in love with you till my last breath
Belongs to you as yours to me

That day my eulogy is read
About all we have accomplished

You as my back bone to my life or
As they say

The good woman behind this evolved

Good man

Then I will know

I was complete....

WILL YOU

Will you take my spirit into your sunray brightening my world?

Will you suspend my soul into the air until I am floating on your cloud nine?

As I follow your rainbow to the pot of gold, only love brings you

While I roll around in your heart of colorful rose petals

Surrounding me in your rainforest of security and love

See I just want to be part of your Moon and Stars

Your land and your crystal blue water

As we lounge in the black sands of romance

I want to be the dream that makes you smile in your sleep

And the night that takes you away from your fears

The type of love that makes a man so secure that he cries on your shoulder

And can scream out "I Love You" through the galaxies above

I want to share the type of love that makes Cupid jealous

That love that makes Angels sing in harmony

Will you be that song that sings me into a peaceful sleep?

WILL YOU

Or just the nightlight that protects me from the dark

Everyone has a soul mate

So what I am really asking is....

Will you be mine....

Will you?

FOREVER

I have looked in the mirror and was paralyzed

As my life was replayed through this reflective glass

Focusing on lost love

I begin to feel confronted by what I would call my alter ego

Often feeling incomplete or lonely

With all the excuses of why I seem to remain single

How I have managed to drive away the good women

Never feeling the space of my missing rib

As a man I got to be willing to face my fears

And no longer run from my potential happiness

Fear of hurt, pain, trust and commitment

Can no longer plague my heart leaving me unfulfilled

Walking away from love, leaving unfinished chapters

In my life of love instead creating chaos

Searching for love

I have lost love

Not paying attention to the soul attempting to caress my heart

At the same time damaging souls

FOREVER

As their hearts, I intentionally and unintentionally pierced

I have loved and I have been loved

So if I never find love again I will always have yester (years)

But I won't stop seeking out my Ruth as I will be her Boaz

Her protector, provider, comforter

And we will go before God

And she will be……

    My forever

RANDOM THOUGHT
(BONUS)

I wanna make love to her soul

While her mind orgasms

As between her thighs soak with wetness

Her heart races out of control

I wanna be able to kiss her

Feel the heat before my lips touch hers

When I'm inside of her

I wanna feel like I'm drowning in her juices

I want an erection every time I think of being in you

Orgasmic thoughts of entering her canal

As my juices flow inside of her

I want her to receive me

As our pheromones fills the room…

A 10/2 MOMENT

I cried inside while laughing at myself because
I thought I did enough to make you stay

Hearing you tell me you love me
never once did I think the time
would come for me to ever feel this way

I just knew my arms would always be wrapped
around you keeping you safe and secure

Sweating while working real hard to erase
the image of another man taking a tour

Cringing from the mere thought of another man
receiving your sexual energy

Just months ago I was receiving all of you
as you looked into my eyes saying it was only for me

Those were my meals, my hot baths, and my cuddle nights
that is now all gone

This is now my loneliness and my empty space
that is a house and no longer a home

Crazy pains in my stomach
a hurt in my heart that refuses to subside

Not realizing than that losing you
I would never be the same for that day
 a piece of me died

Long days just became longer
restless nights lingering into
new heart breaking daybreaks

A 10/2 MOMENT

I move forward fighting to keep you out of my mind
just wanting to sleep and not be awake

Just to realize I was another conquered quest
on her bucket list

OUTRO

As always with love there is pain. But don't let your heart reject pure love when love is sent your way. Pure Love is worth the headache that occurs if you believe that eventually that one person will come along and be the medicine to your pain.

Hopefully this reading helps provide insight, racing hearts, smiles, tears and rejoicing to you.

God Bless you and thank you again…..

Black Life

ABOUT THE AUTHOR

BlackLife is the pseudo name for Nolan J. Turner. BlackLife is a native of Detroit, Michigan. He is also a proud product of the Detroit Public School System - Martin Luther King High School (Crusaders).

He developed his love for writing in the late nineties beginning with writing music that later evolved into a love for poetry.

His first book, Black Book, was published in 2008. Pure Love is his second published book and a portion of the proceeds will be donated to Autism. BlackLife's intent with his poetry is to ensure there is a mixture of poems for everyone to enjoy.

To know a person one must know their mind and BlackLife allows you into his mind. His thought for success is "it is not the money that one makes but the work that one completes".

Black Life

www.ingramcontent.com/pod-product-compliance
Lightning Source LLC
Chambersburg PA
CBHW051709090426
42736CB00013B/2617